MAY 2017

The Thumb and His Chum

Tracy Kompelien

Consulting Editor, Diane Craig, M.A./Reading Specialist

ABDO
Publishing Company

Published by ABDO Publishing Company, 4940 Viking Drive, Edina, Minnesota 55435.

Printed in the United States.

Credits
Edited by: Pam Price
Curriculum Coordinator: Nancy Tuminelly
Cover and Interior Design and Production: Mighty Media
Photo and Illustration Credits: BananaStock Ltd., Comstock, Digital Vision, Image 100, Tracy Kompelien, PhotoDisc

Library of Congress Cataloging-in-Publication Data

Kompelien, Tracy, 1975-
    The thumb and his chum / Tracy Kompelien.
       p. cm. -- (Rhyme time)
    Includes index.
    ISBN 1-59197-819-X (hardcover)
    ISBN 1-59197-925-0 (paperback)
    1. English language--Rhyme--Juvenile literature. I. Title. II. Rhyme time (ABDO Publishing Company)

PE1517.K665 2004
428.1'3--dc22
                                                                            2004049109

SandCastle™ books are created by a professional team of educators, reading specialists, and content developers around five essential components that include phonemic awareness, phonics, vocabulary, text comprehension, and fluency. All books are written, reviewed, and leveled for guided reading, early intervention reading, and Accelerated Reader® programs and designed for use in shared, guided, and independent reading and writing activities to support a balanced approach to literacy instruction.

Let Us Know

After reading the book, SandCastle would like you to tell us your stories about reading. What is your favorite page? Was there something hard that you needed help with? Share the ups and downs of learning to read. We want to hear from you! To get posted on the ABDO Publishing Company Web site, send us e-mail at:

sandcastle@abdopub.com

SandCastle Level: Transitional

Words that rhyme do
not have to be spelled the
same. These words rhyme
with each other:

come

numb

crumb

plum

drum

sum

thumb

dumb

yum

gum

Hank, Neil, and their father bang on the drum.

Jill had a great time at the pool.

She was glad her friend Dot had come too.

At the baseball game, Tate blew a bubble with his **gum**.

At dinner Chelsey announced,
"I am so hungry I won't leave
a crumb!"

At the market, Raina asked her
mom to buy an apple, not
a plum.

Martha likes to do her homework.

She doesn't think it's **dumb**.

Julia's math homework was adding numbers together to find the **sum**.

The dentist gave Edie a shot to make her mouth **numb**.

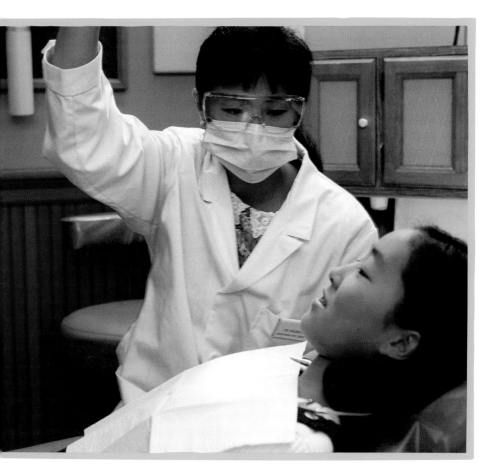

Banana splits are Bradley's favorite dessert.

After every bite, he says, "Yum!"

Linus pushes his helmet up with his **thumb**.

13

The Thumb and His Chum

There once was a giant thumb.
He came from a place called Windom.
His life there was humdrum.

Thumb didn't want
to be a bum.

He was very good
at playing the drum.

He met Jack, who became
his new chum.

Jack liked to sing and strum.

17

Jack and Thumb
decided to become
a band called "The Last Crumb."

They practiced until they were numb.
The sounds they made were awesome!

When The Last Crumb
would strum and drum,
people who were glum
would begin to hum!

19

Thumb wanted to play for his mum.

So Jack and Thumb
went back to Windom.

Once back where he was from,
Thumb was happy and so was his chum.

Everyone made them feel welcome!

Rhyming Riddle

What do you call the total number of cookie pieces?

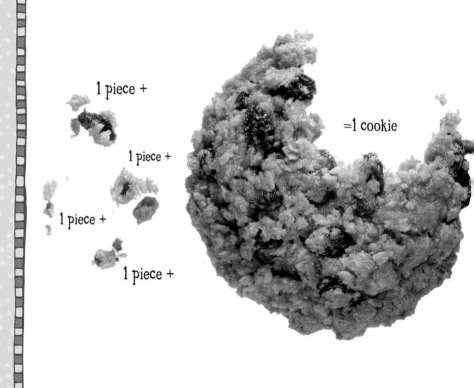

1 piece +

1 piece +

1 piece +

1 piece +

=1 cookie

Crumb sum

Glossary

chum. a close friend or buddy

glum. sad or gloomy

hum. to sing without moving your lips or using words

humdrum. dull or boring

numb. without feeling

strum. to brush the fingertips over the strings of an instrument, such as a guitar

About SandCastle™

A professional team of educators, reading specialists, and content developers created the SandCastle™ series to support young readers as they develop reading skills and strategies and increase their general knowledge. The SandCastle™ series has four levels that correspond to early literacy development in young children. The levels are provided to help teachers and parents select the appropriate books for young readers.

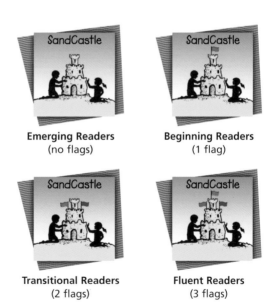

Emerging Readers
(no flags)

Beginning Readers
(1 flag)

Transitional Readers
(2 flags)

Fluent Readers
(3 flags)

These levels are meant only as a guide. All levels are subject to change.

ABDO
Publishing Company

To see a complete list of SandCastle™ books and other nonfiction titles from ABDO Publishing Company, visit www.abdopub.com or contact us at:
4940 Viking Drive, Edina, Minnesota 55435 • 1-800-800-1312 • fax: 1-952-831-1632